MAX LUCADO

P9-CRZ-858

JUST FOR YOU

Readings from *He Chose the Nails*

JUST FOR YOU

MAX LUCADO

W Publishing Group™

www.wpublishinggroup.com

A Division of Thomas Nelson, Inc.
www.ThomasNelson.com

JUST FOR YOU

Copyright © 2001 by Max Lucado.

All rights reserved. No portion of this book may be reproduced, stored in a retrieval system,
or transmitted in any form or by any means—electronic, mechanical, photocopy, recording, or any other—
except for brief quotations in printed reviews, without the prior permission of the publisher.

Published by W Publishing Group, a Division of Thomas Nelson, Inc.,
P.O. Box 141000, Nashville, Tennessee 37214.

Compiled and edited by Nancy Guthrie

THE VISUAL BIBLE
All photos are taken from "Matthew" featuring actor
Bruce Marchiano (Jesus) and the photography of Robby Botha.

These photos are used by permission and are copyrighted by Visual Bible International, Inc. and may not be reproduced without permission.
For more information regarding these photos or The Visual Bible videos call 1-800-33-BIBLE.

Design: Christopher Gilbert/www.uddesignworks.com
Unless otherwise indicated Scripture quotations used in this book are from
the Holy Bible, New Century Version (NCV). Copyright © 1987, 1988, 1991 by Word Publishing,
Dallas, Texas 75234. Used by permission.

Other Scripture references are from the following sources:
The Holy Bible, New Living Translation (NLT), copyright © 1996. Used by permission of Tyndale House Publishers, Inc.,
Wheaton, Illinois 60189. All rights reserved. The Holy Bible, New International Version (NIV). Copyright © 1973, 1978, 1984, International Bible
Society. Used by permission of Zondervan Bible Publishers. The Living Bible (TLB), copyright © 1971 by
Tyndale House Publishers, Wheaton, Ill. Used by permission. The Message (MSG), copyright © 1993. Used by permission of NavPress Publishing
Group. The New King James Version (NKJV), copyright © 1979, 1980, 1982, Thomas Nelson, Inc., Publisher.
The New Revised Standard Version Bible (NRSV), © 1989 by the Division of Christian Education of the National Council of the Churches of Christ
in the USA. The Contemporary English Version (CEV) © 1991 by the American Bible Society. Used by permission. The King James Version of the
Bible (KJV). The New English Bible (NEB),
copyright © 1961, 1970 by the Delegates of Oxford University Press and the Syndics
of the Cambridge University Press, 1961, 1970. Reprinted by permission.

ISBN 0-8499-9044-0

Printed in the United States of America

01 02 03 04 05 PHX 9 8 7 6 5 4 3 2 1

Contents

This is love: not that we loved God,

but that he loved us and sent his

Son as an atoning sacrifice for our sins.

1 JOHN 4:10 NIV

INTRODUCTION

The gifts of the cross.

Much has been said about the gift of the cross itself, but what of the other gifts? What of the nails, the crown of thorns? The garments taken by the soldiers. Have you taken time to open these gifts?

He didn't have to give them, you know. The only act, the only required act for our salvation was the shedding of blood, yet he did much more. So much more. Search the scene of the cross, and what do you find?

A wine-soaked sponge.

A sign.

Two crosses beside Christ.

Divine gifts intended to stir that moment, that split second when your face will brighten, your eyes will widen, as you hear God say to you, "Just for you."

He Became One of You

You know the most amazing thing about the coming of Christ? You know the most remarkable part of the incarnation? Not just that he swapped eternity for calendars. Though such an exchange deserves our notice. Scripture says that the number of God's years is unsearchable (Job 36:26). We may search out the moment the first wave slapped on a shore or the first star burst in the sky, but we'll never find the first moment when God was God, for there is no moment when God was not God. He has never not been, for he is eternal. God is not bound by time.

But when Jesus came to the earth, all this changed. He heard for the first time a phrase never used in heaven: "Your time is up." As a child, he had to leave the Temple because his time was up. As a man, he had to leave Nazareth because his time was up. And as a Savior, he had to die because his time was up. For thirty-three years, the stallion of heaven lived in the corral of time.

That's certainly remarkable, but there is something even more so.

You want to see the brightest jewel in the treasure of incarnation? You might think it was the fact that he lived in a body. One moment he was a boundless spirit; the next he was flesh and bones. When God entered time and became a man, he who was boundless became bound. Imprisoned in flesh. Restricted by weary-prone muscles and eyelids. For more than three decades, his once limitless reach would be limited to the stretch of an arm, his speed checked to the pace of human feet.

And God has reserved for his children

the priceless gift of eternal life;

it is kept in heaven for you, pure and undefiled,

beyond the reach of change and decay.

And God, in his mighty power,

will make sure that you get there safely to receive it,

because you are trusting him.

It will be yours in that coming last day for all to see.

1 PETER 1:4–5 TLB

Not once did Christ use his supernatural powers for personal comfort. With one word he could've transformed the hard earth into a soft bed, but he didn't. With a wave of his hand, he could've boomeranged the spit of his accusers back into their faces, but he didn't. With an arch of his brow, he could've paralyzed the hand of the soldier as he braided the crown of thorns. But he didn't.

Remarkable. But is this the most remarkable part of the coming? Many would argue not. Many, perhaps most, would point beyond the surrender of timelessness and boundlessness to the surrender of sinlessness. It's easy to see why.

Isn't this the message of the crown of thorns?

An unnamed soldier took branches—mature enough to bear thorns, nimble enough to bend—and wove them into a crown of mockery, a crown of thorns. Throughout Scripture thorns symbolize, not sin, but the consequence of sin. Remember Eden? After Adam

and Eve sinned, God cursed the land: "So I will put a curse on the ground. . . . The ground will produce thorns and weeds for you, and you will eat the plants of the field" (Gen. 3:17–18). Brambles on the earth are the product of sin in the heart.

This truth is echoed in God's words to Moses. He urged the Israelites to purge the land of godless people. Disobedience would result in difficulties. "But if you don't force those people out of the land, they will bring you trouble. They will be like sharp hooks in your eyes and thorns in your sides" (Num. 33:55).

Rebellion results in thorns. "Evil people's lives are like paths covered with thorns and traps" (Prov. 22:5). Jesus even compared the lives of evil people to a thornbush. In speaking of false prophets, he said, "You will know these people by what they do. Grapes don't come from thornbushes, and figs don't come from thorny weeds" (Matt. 7:16).

The fruit of sin is thorns—spiny, prickly, cutting thorns. I emphasize the "point" of the thorns to suggest a point you may have never considered: If the fruit of sin is thorns, isn't the thorny crown on Christ's brow a picture of the fruit of our sin that pierced his heart?

What is the fruit of sin? Step into the briar patch of humanity and feel a few thistles. Shame. Fear. Disgrace. Discouragement. Anxiety. Haven't our hearts been caught in these brambles?

The heart of Jesus, however, had not. He had never been cut by the thorns of sin. What you and I face daily, he never knew. Anxiety? He never worried! Guilt? He was never guilty! Fear? He never left the presence of God! Jesus never knew the fruits of sin . . . until he became sin for us.

And when he did, all the emotions of sin tumbled in on him like shadows in a forest. He felt anxious, guilty, and alone. Can't you hear the emotion in his prayer? "My God, my God, why have you rejected me?" (Matt. 27:46). These are not the words of a saint. This is the cry of a sinner.

And this prayer is one of the most remarkable parts of his coming. But I can think of something even greater. Want to know what it is? Want to know the coolest thing about the coming?

Not that he, in an instant, went from needing nothing to needing air, food, a tub of hot water and salts for his tired feet, and, more than anything, needing somebody—anybody—who was more concerned about where he would spend eternity than where he would spend Friday's paycheck.

Or that he resisted the urge to fry the two-bit, self-appointed hall monitors of holiness who dared suggest that he was doing the work of the devil.

Not that he kept his cool while the dozen best friends he ever had felt the heat and got out of the kitchen. Not that he refused to defend himself when blamed for every sin of every slut and sailor since Adam. Or that he stood silent as a million guilty verdicts echoed in the tribunal of heaven and the giver of light was left in the chill of a sinner's night.

Not even that after three days in a dark hole he stepped into the Easter sunrise with a smile and a swagger and a question for lowly Lucifer—"Is that your best punch?"

That was cool, incredibly cool.

But want to know the coolest thing about the One who gave up the crown of heaven for a crown of thorns?

He did it for you. Just for you.

You were bought, not with something that

ruins like gold or silver, but with the precious blood

of Christ, who was like a pure and perfect lamb.

Christ was chosen before the world was made,

but he was shown to the world in

these last times for your sake.

1 PETER 1:18-20

He forgave all our sins.

He canceled the debt, which listed all the

rules we failed to follow.

He took away that record with its

rules and nailed it to the cross.

COLOSSIANS 2:13–14

He Covered
Your Sins

Would you like anyone to see the list of your weaknesses? Would you like them made public? How would you feel if they were posted high so that everyone, including Christ himself, could see?

May I take you to the moment it was? Yes, there is a list of your failures. Christ has chronicled your shortcomings. And, yes, that list has been made public. But you've never seen it. Neither have I.

Come with me to the hill of Calvary, and I'll tell you why.

Watch as the soldiers shove the Carpenter to the ground and stretch his arms against the beams. One presses a knee against a forearm and a spike against a hand. Jesus turns his face toward the nail just as the soldier lifts the hammer to strike it.

Couldn't Jesus have stopped him? With a flex of the biceps, with a clench of the fist, he could have resisted. Is this not the same hand that stilled the sea? Cleansed the Temple? Summoned the dead?

But the fist doesn't clench . . . and the moment isn't aborted.

The mallet rings and the skin rips and the blood begins to drip, then rush. Then the questions follow. Why? Why didn't Jesus resist?

"Because he loved us," we reply. That is true, wonderfully true, but—forgive me—only partially true. There is more to his reason. He saw something that made him stay. As the soldier pressed his arm, Jesus rolled his head to the side, and with his cheek resting on the wood he saw:

A mallet? Yes.

A nail? Yes.

The soldier's hand? Yes.

But he saw something else. He saw the hand of God. It appeared to be the hand of a man.

Long fingers of a woodworker. Callous palms of a carpenter. It appeared common. It was, however, anything but.

These fingers formed Adam out of clay and furrowed truth into tablets.

With a wave, this hand toppled Babel's tower and split the Red Sea.

From this hand flew the locusts that plagued Egypt and the raven that fed Elijah.

Is it any wonder the psalmist celebrated liberation by declaring: "You drove out the nations with Your hand. . . . It was Your right hand,

Your arm, and the light of Your countenance" (Ps. 44:2–3 NKJV).

The hand of God is a mighty hand.

They couldn't see it. But Jesus could. And heaven could. And we can.

Through the eyes of Scripture we see what others missed but what Jesus saw. "He canceled the record that contained the charges against us. He took it and destroyed it by nailing it to Christ's cross" (Col. 2:14 NLT).

Between his hand and the wood there was a list. A long list. A list of our mistakes: our lusts and lies and greedy moments and prodigal years. A list of our sins.

Dangling from the cross is an itemized catalog of your sins. The bad decisions from last year. The bad attitudes from last week. There, in broad daylight for all of heaven to see, is a list of your mistakes.

God has penned a list of our faults. The list God has made,

You drove out the nations

with Your hand. . . . It was Your

right hand, Your arm, and the

light of Your countenance.

P S A L M   4 4 : 2 – 3   N K J V

however, cannot be read. The words can't be deciphered. The mistakes are covered. The sins are hidden. Those at the top are hidden by his hand; those down the list are covered by his blood. Your sins are "blotted out" by Jesus.

This is why he refused to close his fist. He saw the list! What kept him from resisting? This warrant, this tabulation of your failures. He knew the price of those sins was death. He knew the source of those sins was you, and since he couldn't bear the thought of eternity without you, he chose the nails.

The hand squeezing the handle was not a Roman infantryman.

The force behind the hammer was not an angry mob.

The verdict behind the death was not decided by jealous Jews.

Jesus himself chose the nails.

So the hands of Jesus opened up. Had the soldier hesitated, Jesus himself would have swung the mallet. He knew how; he was no stranger to the driving of nails. As a carpenter he knew what it took. And as a Savior he knew what it meant. He knew that the purpose of the nail was to place your sins where they could be hidden by his sacrifice and covered by his blood.

So Jesus himself swung the hammer.

The same hand that stilled the seas stills your guilt.

The same hand that cleansed the Temple cleanses your heart.

The hand is the hand of God.

The nail is the nail of God.

And as the hands of Jesus opened for the nail, the doors of heaven opened for you.

For he has rescued us

from the dominion of darkness

and brought us into the kingdom of

the Son he loves.

COLOSSIANS 1:13 NIV

You have all put on Christ as a garment.

GALATIANS 3:27 NEB

HE ROBED YOU
in HIS
RIGHTEOUSNESS

*S*eats at God's table are not available to the sloppy. But who among us is anything but? Unkempt morality. Untidy with truth. Careless with people. Our moral clothing is in disarray. Yes, the standard for sitting at God's table is high, but the love of God for his children is higher. So he offers a gift, a robe. A seamless robe. A robe worn by his Son, Jesus.

Scripture says little about the clothes Jesus wore. We know what his cousin John the Baptist wore. We know what the religious leaders wore. But the clothing of Christ is nondescript: neither so humble as to touch hearts nor so glamorous as to turn heads.

One reference to Jesus' garments is noteworthy. "They divided his clothes among the four of them. They also took his robe, but it was seamless, woven in one piece from the top. So they said, 'Let's not tear it but throw dice to see who gets it'" (John 19:23–24 NLT).

It must have been Jesus' finest possession. Jewish tradition called for a mother to make such a robe and present it to her son as a departure gift when he left home. Had Mary done this for Jesus? We don't know. But we do know the tunic was without seam, woven from top to bottom. Why is this significant?

Scripture often describes our behavior as the clothes we wear. Peter urges us to be "clothed with humility" (1 Pet. 5:5 NKJV). David speaks of evil people who clothe themselves "with cursing" (Ps. 109:18 NKJV). Garments can symbolize character, and like his garment, Jesus' character was seamless. Coordinated. Unified. He was like his robe: uninterrupted perfection.

"Woven . . . from the top"(John 19:23 NLT). Jesus wasn't led by his own mind; he was led by the mind of his Father. Listen to his words:

"The Son can do nothing on his own, but only what he sees the Father doing; for whatever the Father does, the Son does likewise" (John 5:19 NRSV).

"I can do nothing on my own. As I hear, I judge" (John 5:30 NRSV).

The character of Jesus was a seamless fabric woven from heaven to earth . . . from God's thoughts to Jesus' actions. From God's tears to Jesus' compassion. From God's word to Jesus' response. All one piece. All a picture of the character of Jesus.

But when Christ was nailed to the cross, he took off his robe of seamless perfection and assumed a different wardrobe, the wardrobe of indignity.

The indignity of nakedness. Stripped before his own mother and loved ones. Shamed before his family.

The indignity of failure. For a few pain-filled hours, the religious leaders were the victors, and Christ appeared the loser. Shamed before his accusers.

Worst of all, he wore the indignity of sin. "He himself bore our sins in his body on the tree, so that we might die to sins and live for righteousness" (I Pet. 2:24 NIV).

The clothing of Christ on the cross? Sin—yours and mine. The sins of all humanity.

While on the cross, Jesus felt the indignity and disgrace of a criminal. No, he was not guilty. No, he had not committed a sin. And, no, he

The Son can do nothing on his own,

but only what he sees the Father doing;

for whatever the Father does,

the Son does likewise.

JOHN 5:19 NRSV

did not deserve to be sentenced. But you and I were, we had, and we did.

"He changed places with us" (Gal. 3:13). He wore our sin so we could wear his righteousness.

Though we come to the cross dressed in sin, we leave the cross dressed in the "coat of his strong love" (Isa. 59:17) and girded with a belt of "goodness and fairness" (Isa. 11:5) and clothed in "garments of salvation" (Isa. 61:10 NIV).

Indeed, we leave dressed in Christ himself.

It wasn't enough for him to prepare you a feast.

It wasn't enough for him to reserve you a seat.

It wasn't enough for him to cover the cost and provide the transportation to the banquet.

He did something more. He let you wear his own clothes so that you would be properly dressed.

He did that . . . because he loved you enough.

For Christ died for sins once for all,

the righteous for the unrighteous,

to bring you to God.

1 PETER 3:18 NIV

HE KEEPS YOU SAFE
IN THE SHADOW OF
THE CROSS

*H*ow is it that God can be both just and kind?

How can he dispense truth and mercy?

How can he redeem the sinner without endorsing the sin?

Can a holy God overlook our mistakes?

Can a kind God punish our mistakes?

From our perspective there are only two equally unappealing solutions. But from his perspective there is a third. It's called "the Cross of Christ."

The cross. Can you turn any direction without seeing one? Perched atop a chapel. Carved into a graveyard headstone. Engraved in a ring or suspended on a chain. The cross is the universal symbol of Christianity. An odd choice, don't you think? Strange that a tool of torture would come to embody a movement of hope. The symbols of other faiths are more upbeat: the six-pointed Star of David, the crescent moon of Islam, a lotus blossom for Buddhism. Yet a cross for Christianity? An instrument of execution?

Would you wear a tiny electric chair around your neck? Suspend a gold-plated hangman's noose on the wall? Would you print a picture of a firing squad on a business card? Yet we do so with the cross. Many even make the sign of the cross as they pray. Would we make the sign of, say, a guillotine? Instead of the triangular touch on the forehead and shoulders, how about a karate chop on the palm? Doesn't quite have the same feel, does it?

Why is the cross the symbol of our faith? To find the answer look no farther than the cross itself. Its design couldn't be simpler. One beam horizontal—the other vertical. One reaches out—like God's love. The other reaches up—as does God's holiness. One represents the width of his love; the other reflects the height of his holiness. The cross is the intersection. The cross is where God forgave his children without lowering his standards.

How could he do this? In a sentence: God put our sin on his Son and punished it there.

"God put on him the wrong who never did anything wrong, so we could be put right with God" (2 Cor. 5:21 MSG).

Or as rendered elsewhere: "Christ never sinned! But God treated him as a sinner, so that Christ could make us acceptable to God" (CEV).

Envision the moment. God on his throne. You on the earth. And between you and God, suspended between you and heaven, is Christ

For God so loved the world

that he gave his one and only Son,

that whoever believes in him shall not perish

but have eternal life.

JOHN 3:16 NIV

on his cross. Your sins have been placed on Jesus. God, who punishes sin, releases his rightful wrath on your mistakes. Jesus receives the blow. Since Christ is between you and God, you don't. The sin is punished, but you are safe—safe in the shadow of the cross.

This is what God did, but why, why would he do it? Moral duty? Heavenly obligation? Paternal requirement? No. God is required to do nothing.

Besides, consider what he did. He gave his Son. His only Son. Would you do that? Would you offer the life of your child for someone else? I wouldn't. There are those for whom I would give my life. But ask me to make a list of those for whom I would kill my daughter? The sheet will be blank. I don't need a pencil. The list has no names.

But God's list contains the name of every person who ever lived. For this is the scope of his love. And this is the reason for the cross. He loves the world.

God was in Christ

reconciling the world to Himself.

2 C O R I N T H I A N S   5 : 1 9   N K J V

"For God so loved the world that he gave his only Son" (John 3:16 NLT).

As boldly as the center beam proclaims God's holiness, the cross-beam declares his love. And, oh, how wide his love reaches.

Aren't you glad the verse does not read:

"For God so loved the rich . . . "?

Or, "For God so loved the famous . . . "?

Or, "For God so loved the thin . . . "?

It doesn't. Nor does it state, "For God so loved the Europeans or Africans . . . ," "the sober or successful . . . ," "the young or the old . . ."

No, when we read John 3:16, we simply (and happily) read, "For God so loved the world."

How wide is God's love? Wide enough for the whole world. Are you included in the world? Then you are included in God's love.

It's nice to be included. You aren't always. Universities exclude you

if you aren't smart enough. Businesses exclude you if you aren't qualified enough, and, sadly, some churches exclude you if you aren't good enough.

But though they may exclude you, Christ includes you.

But isn't there a limit? Surely there has to be an end to this love. You'd think so, wouldn't you? But David the adulterer never found it. Paul the murderer never found it. Peter the liar never found it. When it came to life, they hit bottom. But when it came to God's love, they never did.

They, like you, found their names on God's list of love.

When asked to describe the width of his love, he stretched one hand to the right and the other to the left and had them nailed in that position so you would know he died loving you.

But God demonstrates

his own love for us in this:

While we were still sinners,

Christ died for us.

ROMANS 5:8 NIV

When asked to describe the width of his love

He stretched one hand to the right and the other to the

left and had them nailed in that position so you

would know he died

...loving you.

Not only is this so, but we also rejoice

in God through our Lord Jesus Christ,

through whom we have now received reconciliation.

ROMANS 3:11 NIV